Louise
Park

art attack

Programmed art for the frenzied teacher

ASHTON SCHOLASTIC
Sydney Auckland New York Toronto London

Park, Louise.
Art attack: programmed art for the frenzied teacher.

ISBN 0 86896 395 X.

1. Art - Study and teaching (Elementary).
I. Title.

372.5'044

First published in 1988 by Ashton Scholastic Pty Limited (Inc. in
NSW), PO Box 579, Gosford 2250. Also in Brisbane, Melbourne,
Adelaide, Perth and Auckland, NZ.

Designed by Tina Smith
Photography by Ken Dolling
Typeset by Dovatype
Printed in Hong Kong

12 11 10 9 8 7 6 5   0 / 9

contents

introduction

It's all been said and done before so what's so different about this book?

In teaching you don't have time to search through a stack of books to construct and write an art program on paper - a book on art theory, one on materials, one on method and so on. You want to be able to find a working model and implement it immediately from aims and objectives through to evaluation. This book gives you just that - a working model which slips easily into your program and is skill based.

The art activities in this book have been arranged in a unit format so that you can immediately use them as a program to work from. Each unit deals with a skill or medium and demonstrates how a developmentally skill-based unit can be approached in the classroom. All the activities are simple, easy to conduct and require little preparation.

Most units in this book can be adapted to any grade by either simplifying or extending the activity and, although the activities are arranged progressively in both skill and acquisition of knowledge, you can select and arrange a unit from these which may more readily suit your class - for this reason the aims and objectives accompanying these units are very broad and general.

Some helpful hints on evaluation have been included at the back of the book which may come in handy at the completion of the unit and evaluating your program as well as your class. Above all this book is designed to generate fun experiences in the classroom as well as giving children the opportunity to gain confidence and express themselves freely.

Remember, a sound art program should encourage creativity, stimulate language, develop aesthetic skills, enable plenty of experimentation, act as a vehicle for self-expression, reinforce a positive self-concept, aid in the development of physical co-ordination, and give a feeling of joy.

paintworks

5

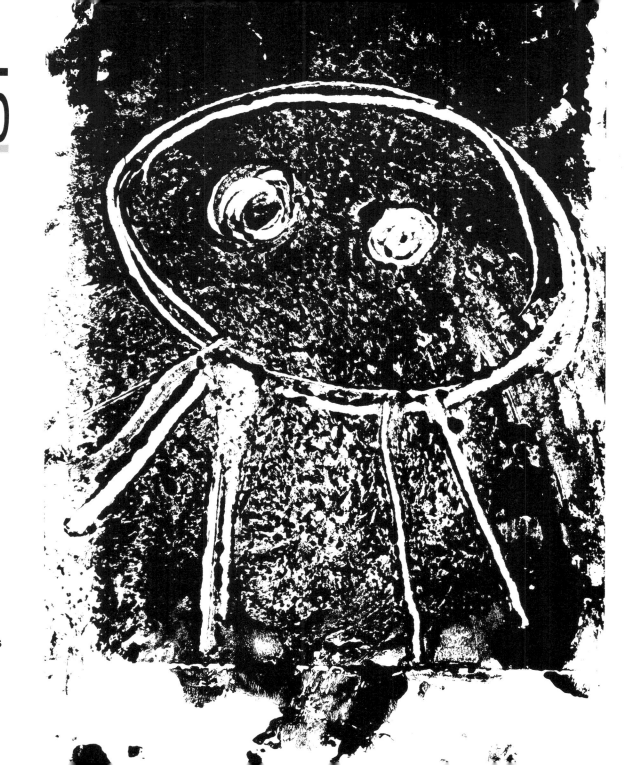

Aim

To involve the child in as many varied
activities in the use of paint as possible
in an effort to explore a number of
painting techniques.

General objectives

■ To develop skill in the handling and
care of a paintbrush
■ To be able to explore and experiment
with a variety of painting techniques
■ To explore painting styles using
unusual media and tools.
■ To gain expertise in the skills
associated with the various techniques
■ To demonstrate both joy and
confidence whilst implementing these
skills
Refer to evaluation checklist, page 93,
for ideas on evaluating the unit.

Wet painting

What you need:

waterpaints
water
brushes
paper

What to do:

1 Wet the page entirely, either with your paint brush or by holding it under a trickle of water.
2 Paint your picture onto the wet page and watch the effects before your very eyes.

String painting

What you need:

string
paper ·
newspaper
paint

What to do:

1 Lay a sheet of paper on a pile of old newspapers.
2 Saturate your string with paint.

3 Lay this on the paper in an interesting manner.
4 Leave both ends dangling over the edges and cover this with another sheet of paper, followed by more newspaper.
5 Ask a friend to hold everything down firmly whilst you very quickly pull both ends of the string tight.
6 Open the pages to reveal an interesting design.

Spatter work

What you need:

old toothbrushes
paint
paper

What to do:

1 Cut your shape out of paper.
2 Lay this on a larger, blank page.
3 Load your toothbrush with paint.
4 Now flick the paint all over the page until you are pleased with the coverage.
5 This can also be done with a spray-can.
6 Now lift up the shape and expose your pattern.

Wash offs

What you need:

white tempera paint
paper
black ink
brushes

What to do:

1 Paint a scene in white tempera.
2 Allow this to dry.
3 Paint over the entire page with black
  ink.
4 When it is dry, run the page under water.
5 The ink will stick to the blank paper
  leaving the white picture exposed.

Shape paint

What you need:

cardboard
paint
brushes
paper

What to do:

1 Cut out a simple shape from
  cardboard.

2 Position this on your page and hold it
  very still.
3 Carefully paint around the shape and
  then lift it to expose the print.
4 Continue doing this until you have
  covered the page in an all-over
  pattern.

Straw blowing

What you need:

drinking straw
paper
ink or runny paint

What to do:

1 Using an eyedropper or the straw,
  drop a few colours onto your page in
  a variety of places.
2 Holding the straw approximately 1 cm
  from the page, blow through the
  straw in the direction you want the
  paint to go.
3 Allow this to dry flat.

Wax resist painting

What you need:

paint, ink
water
brushes
old candle pieces, crayons,
 rubber cement
paper

What to do:

1 Draw your design on the paper with the candle.
2 Paint over your design in brightly coloured paints or ink to expose the design.
3 Allow to dry.
4 Discuss with the group the implications of the paint leaving the wax.

Use paint that is runny but not watery.

The candle pieces can also be melted and the design drawn with a paintbrush.

If using rubber cement, rub it off the paper to leave the design. More cement can then be added and the process repeated to create a multi-coloured design.

Water pictures

What you need:

water
very watered-down paint
black paint, ink or pens

What to do:

1 Run a blank page under a tap.
2 Whilst wet, drop a few colours onto the page and juggle the paper around to make them run in effective ways.
3 For this you need hardly any paint, just coloured water - try to cover as much of the page as possible.
4 When this is dry look for a hidden scene or creature.
5 Start going over this with the black paint or ink to create a picture.

Bubble pictures

What you need:

1/2 cup soap flakes
1/2 cup water
detergent
stirrer
drinking straws
bowl
hand mixer
paint or food colouring
paper
containers

What to do:

Method one
1 Beat the flakes and water until they are stiff.
2 Divide the mixture up into as many cups as the number of colours you plan to have.
3 Add the appropriate food colouring to each container and stir.
4 Paint your picture with the bubbles and let it stand overnight.

Method two
1 Pour the detergent into a container and add enough paint to give a strong colour.
2 Using a straw, blow into the container until bubbles rise about 3 cm over the edge.
3 When the bubbles begin to fall over the side, stop blowing and roll your paper gently over the top.
4 Continue in this manner with as many colours as you like and lay flat to dry so as not to burst the bubbles.

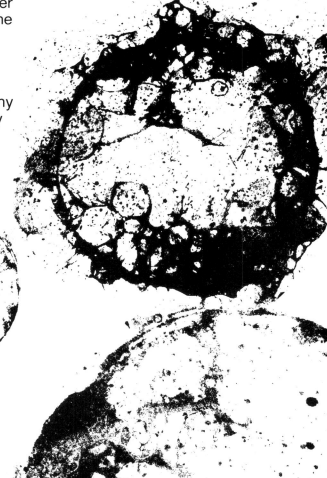

Cotton bud painting

What you need:

cotton buds
paint
paper

What to do:

1 Decide on a design which is suitable for your page.
2 Dip the cotton bud into the paint and draw with it as you would with a pencil.
3 Make sure you keep your cotton buds separate in colours.

Glue and sand painting

What you need:

sand
paint or food colouring
containers
glue
paper

What to do:

1 Divide the sand up into the same number of jars as there are to be colours.
2 Mix some food colouring or paint into the sand and shake the jar until the sand is coloured.
3 Using the glue, paint your design onto the page.
4 Before the glue dries cover the areas with the coloured sands.

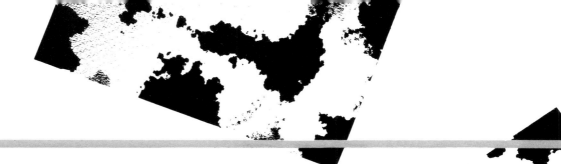

Dip and dye folds

What you need:

food colouring or watery paint
containers
absorbent paper
pegs (optional)

What to do:

1 Fold a sheet of absorbent paper
  repeatedly until it is quite small.
2 Attach a peg to hold on to while you
  dip a corner into the dye.
3 Hold the paper in the food colouring
  for a few seconds to allow it time to
  soak up the dye.
4 Immerse the other corners in various
  colours using the same procedure.
5 Open the paper out carefully and
  hang to dry.
6 A variation on this would be to cut a
  pattern into the fold before dipping.

Tube painting

What you need:

flour
salt
paint
heavy paper or cardboard
plastic squeeze bottles

What to do:

1 Mix up equal parts of flour and salt.
  Add enough paint to form a runny
  paste.
2 Pour this into the bottles and squeeze
  out a design onto the page.
3 While the paint is still wet you could
  sprinkle on some glitter.

chalk
it up to experience

Chalk is possibly the most abundant medium which can be used in the classroom today. It is an excellent tool for all grades which allows the child to create a variety of textures, effects and colours in a small area with little preparation and clean up afterwards. So why not exploit it in your classroom.

Aim

To investigate chalk as an art medium in a wide variety of conditions.

General objectives

- To gain expertise in using chalk in a variety of ways
- To encourage experimentation with a familiar medium
- To enable the development of graduated skills through chalk as the art medium
- To explore the various properties of chalk as a medium

Texture rubbings

What you need:

paper
chalk
a variety of textures
hairspray

What to do:

1 Allow the children to find a surface with an interesting texture.
2 Hold the paper against this and rub the chalk over it.
3 Place the paper over another texture and repeat the process.
4 Spray the picture with hairspray to preserve the chalk.

Textures can be overlapped or blended in together around the edges to give added effect.

Crayons may be used instead of chalk.

Dusting

What you need:

chalk
ruler or flat blunt instrument
cotton balls (optional)

What to do:

1 Draw your picture to be coloured with the chalk.
2 Scrape the chalk along the edge with the tool chosen.
3 Allow the dust produced from this friction to settle in the appropriate spot on your page.
4 This can be rubbed around lightly either with your finger or the cotton balls, to colour the appropriate spot.

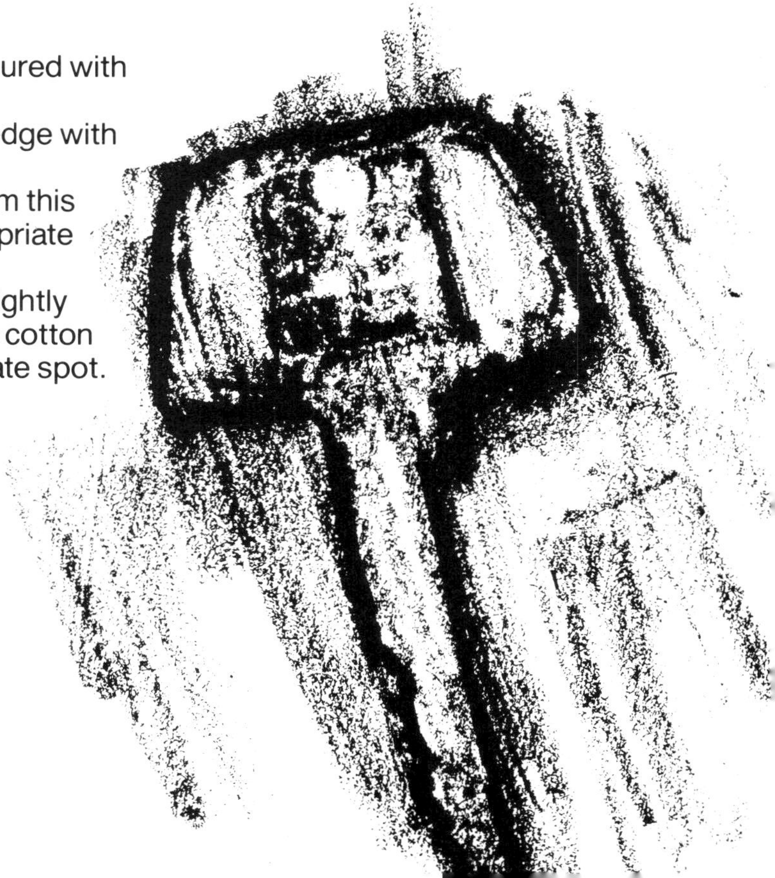

Sugar chalk

What you need:

paper
coloured chalk
sugar
water
paper towel or newspaper

What to do:

1 Mix 1 part water with 2 parts sugar in a container.
2 Immerse the chalk in the solution for approximately 10 minutes.
3 Take these out and leave them on some paper towels.
4 Use the chalk to create designs, patterns and pictures.

Wet chalk

What you need:

brightly coloured chalk
wet paper

What to do:

Draw on a sheet of wet paper with a piece of coloured chalk and watch the colours come alive.

A successful combination of both dry and wet chalk can be achieved by only wetting parts of the paper with a paint brush.

Marbled chalk

What you need:

paper or typing paper
coloured chalk
a blunt knife
a tray filled with water
hairspray (optional)

What to do:

1 Scrape off flakes of chalk with the knife allowing the flakes to fall on the surface of the water.
2 Lay your paper down on the surface of the water but do not immerse it.
3 Lift it out and allow it to dry.
4 This can then be sprayed with hairspray to fix the chalk.

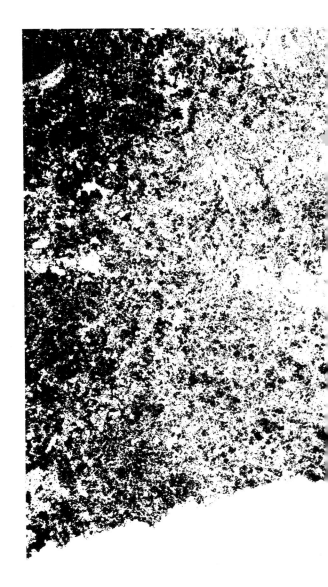

Chalk and Tempera

What you need:

paper
chalk
Tempera paint
hairspray (optional)

What to do:

1 Draw your design or picture very lightly on a piece of paper.
2 Mix up some paint to a creamy consistency.
3 Dip the chalk into the paint and trace over your drawing.

A variation of this is to cover the page with white paint and draw into this with coloured chalk to create pastel effects.

Chalk and starch

What you need:

paper
coloured chalk
liquid starch

What to do:

1 Make your picture or design using the chalk.
2 Using your fingers, paint your design with the starch.

A variation of this is to cover the page with starch and draw into the wet surface with the chalk.

A salt sculpture

What you need:

coloured chalk
a glass or clear container with a lid
a box of salt for each child
a spoon
paper towels
a cup for each different coloured chalk

What to do:

1 Select the colours that you want to use.
2 Put some salt on a paper towel and rub the chalk over it continuously until the salt is the desired shade.
3 Place the coloured salt in a cup until you are ready to use it.
4 Repeat this process for each different colour required.
5 Pour the salt into the glass container one colour at a time. Be careful not to knock the jar while you are filling it.
6 Fill the jar and allow the salt to settle by leaving it to stand for a while.
7 Add more salt and close the container tightly.

For an interesting effect, pour the salt in uneven layers.

let's print it

Aim

To involve the child in a number of graded printing activities which will enable them to investigate, explore and master the relevant skills involved in the printing process.

General objectives

- To gain expertise in the making of a simple print
- To experience a wide variety of media and tools in the process of making different prints
- To create a learning atmosphere which will give the child both confidence and joy
- To acquire the relevant skills involved in printing techniques

Monoprints

What you need:

a laminex table or small sheet of plastic
water paints
paper
fingers and other drawing tools

What to do:

1 Cover the surface of the table with
   whatever colour paint you have
   chosen.
2 Using your finger, draw your design
   through the paint. Make sure that
   your finger is removing the paint.
3 Gently lay a piece of paper over this
   and carefully press down making
   sure that you do not move the paper.
4 Carefully peel back the paper to
   expose the print.

Laying a wet piece of paper over your
design will often ensure an excellent
print.

Another activity which teaches the
printing principle is blob prints. See
page 47 for instructions.

Ink marbles

What you need:

water-based drawing inks
paint brushes or eyedropper
plastic or any other easy-to-clean
surface

What to do:

1 Using either an eyedropper or a paint
   brush, place a few drops of ink on the
   glass.
2 Gently lay the paper over the glass.
3 Peel the paper back slowly to expose
   the print.

Magazine prints

What you need:

old magazines
scissors
turpentine
paper
pencils
brushes
rollers or sponges

What to do:

1 Cut out a clear picture from a magazine.
2 Place the picture face down on the paper.
3 Now paint the back of the picture with turpentine.
4 Whilst the back is still wet, scribble evenly and firmly over this.
5 Carefully pull the picture away and you should have the print of it on your paper.

Roller printing

What you need:

kitchen sponges
thick paint or printing ink
rollers
paper

What to do:

1 Cut a pattern into the sponge.
2 Wrap the sponge around the roller and secure it firmly.
3 Roll the sponge through paint until it is fully coated.
4 Roll the sponge across your paper to create interesting patterns.

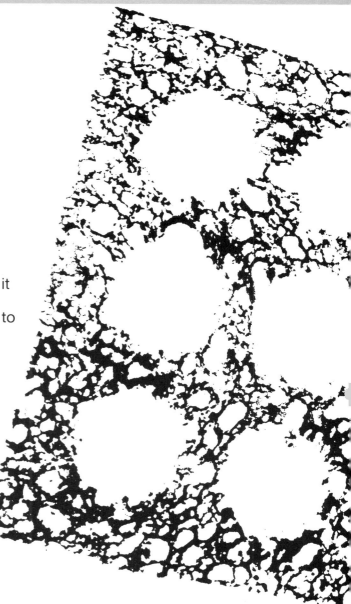

Foam prints

What you need:

polystrene trays
blunt pencils
thick tempera or water-based printing ink
roller (optional)

What to do:

1 Use the blunt pencil to press a design into the tray.
2 Roll the paint on to the tray so as not to fill in the etched drawing.
3 Lay the paper down and roll over it evenly.
4 Peel the page back to expose the design.

Lino prints

What you need:

old lino offcuts
lino-cutting tools
printing ink
paper

What to do:

This technique is the same as foam printing except that you etch your design into the lino with special cutting tools. Once this is done you can obtain a print using the same method as foam printing.

Marbling

What you need:

paper
marbling inks or oil paint
turpentine
water
long dish (a square cake tray is perfect)

What to do:

1 Fill the dish with water.
2 Drop a few different coloured inks or paints onto the water surface.
3 Swirl them around into an interesting pattern.
4 Lay a sheet of paper onto the water. Do not immerse.
5 Gently lift the paper out and allow it to dry.

If you are using oil paint, use approximately 2 cm of paint to half a cup of turpentine. Keep this in an airtight container.

Eyedroppers are useful for dropping the paint onto the water.

Remember, try to lift, not drag, the paper from the water.

Silk-screen prints

What you need:

silk screens
squeegee
printing ink
paper
scissors

What to do:

1 Cut out the design you want printed on paper.
2 Lay this on top of another sheet.
3 Place the screen over both sheets and load with a strip of paint down one side of the screen.
4 Use the squeegee to drag the paint across the screen.
5 Lift up the screen and carefully remove your cut-out shape to expose your print.

Keep your shape as well and you will have a positive and negative display.

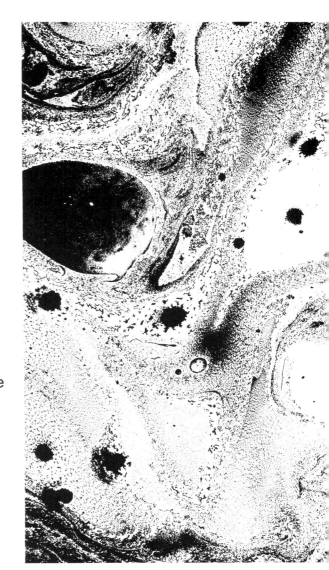

Nature prints

What you need:

a textured surface
paint
paper

What to do:

1 Lightly paint the textured surface or press it into a sponge soaked with paint.
2 Press this down on to scrap paper first to remove any excess paint.
3 Print onto your page any way you like.

the crayon

Crayon is another medium which is readily available in the classroom. It offers a number of properties to be explored by children and this unit is designed to take both the teacher and the child through a number of graduated skill based activities. It is a relatively inexpensive medium and can be melted down into paint when the pieces are too small to use as a writing implement so there is absolutely no waste factor.

Aim

To expose the child to the crayon as an art medium under a wide variety of conditions.

General objectives

■ To explore the crayon as a medium for expression
■ To acquire the relevant skills involved in the exploitation of the crayon's many properties
■ To develop increased skill in the handling of the crayon

The first activity for this unit is texture rubbings. See page 13 for instructions.

Blending

What you need:

wax crayons
paper
old newspapers
erasers

What to do:

1 The children can either colour a picture or just colour the page by placing one colour alongside the next whilst overlapping these slightly.
2 The colours are then blended by rubbing an eraser quickly over the page.

Interesting effects can be obtained by doing the rubbing on a stack of old newspapers.

Stencilling

What you need:

crayons
scissors
cardboard
paper

What to do:

1 Draw an interesting shape onto the cardboard and cut it out.
2 Place the shape on the page and hold it down firmly.
3 Drag the crayon over the shape and onto the page so that, when it is lifted, the impression of the shape is left.
4 Repeat this process over the whole page to produce a design.

Children can cut out shapes from old Christmas cards to use as stencils. Try to keep the stencil designs as simple as possible and remember you will only get the outside shape.

Transfers

What you need:

wax crayons
paper

What to do:

1 Allow the child to do a design or colour in the page with crayons.
2 Place the design face down on to blank paper.
3 Draw on the reverse side with a pencil and the drawing will be transferred.

The more pressure applied to the back of the paper the better the transfer will be.

Another way of doing this and to save paper is to fold the page in half and only draw on one side.

Etchings

What you need:

crayons
paint
brushes
paper
combs, sticks and so on to use as etching tools

What to do:

1 Colour the entire page with brightly coloured crayons.
2 Cover the page with a thick coating of dark paint.
3 Choose an etching tool and scratch patterns through the paint. This will lift the paint and expose a bright crayon design underneath.

Once the paper is dry the children can also scratch a design into the page using a sharp instrument.

Fabric work

What you need:

wax crayons
fabric remnants
paper
warm iron

What to do:

1 Get the children to draw directly onto the material or plan their drawing on paper first. They can use any of the techniques already acquired.
2 Press the cloth between two sheets of paper with a warm iron.

Ironing the fabric between sheets of paper tends to make the crayon permanent.

Crayon melts

What you need:

crayon shavings
wax paper
iron
newspaper
art paper

What to do:

1 Make sure the page is resting on a few sheets of newspaper.
2 Sprinkle some brightly coloured crayon shavings onto the page where you would like that colour to be.
3 When you are happy with the arrangement of colour, lay a sheet of wax paper over this, followed by a sheet of newspaper.
4 Press gently with a warm iron.

Encaustic paint

Encaustic paint is the best way to use up all of those little pieces of crayon that you would normally throw out. When kept in an airtight jar it will continue to go forever, the reason being that as it hardens it requires turpentine to be added to restore it to its liquid state thus doubling the bulk each time you do this. And it will keep forever!

What you need:

wax crayons
paper
brushes
turpentine
rags
cake trays

What to do:

Method one
1 Melt crayon shavings in the cake tray.
2 Using a paint brush, paint directly onto the paper.

This will give you the brightest colours and best textures possible.

Method two
1 Create your pattern or design on the page with crayons.
2 Put a small amount of turpentine on a rag and drag the rag over the page. The turpentine will melt the crayon, giving a smudging effect.

The more turpentine you use the greater the effect will be.

Method three
1 Melt crayons over a low heat.
2 Add turpentine to the melted crayons until the mixture is creamy.
3 This mixture can be painted directly onto paper.

magazines

The weird artist uses magazines

Aim

To explore the many uses magazines
have in an art program.

General objectives

■ To gain confidence in basic weaving
skills
■ To experiment with a variety of
montage techniques
■ To express themselves freely through
the use of collage
■ To develop an awareness of texture
and colour through the use of magazine
cuttings

Weaving paper

What you need:

a magazine picture
plain paper
scissors

What to do:

1 Cut a piece of plain paper the same size as the magazine picture.
2 Fold the magazine picture in half and cut approximately 1 cm strips to about 3 cm from the edge.
3 Weave the plain sheet of paper through the slits in the picture.

OR

Cut the plain sheet into 1 cm strips and weave these through the slits in the picture.

Try cutting the paper in wavy strips to weave through the straight ones.

Magazine mosaic work

What you need:

magazines
glue
scissors
backing paper

What to do:

1 Decide on your picture and draw this clearly onto your backing paper.
2 Now choose which colours best suit your drawing and where they should go.
3 Look in magazines for pieces of photos in these colours, cut or tear them out in bits.
4 Colour your design by gluing all the coloured pieces of the photo onto your drawing.

Magazine letters

What you need:

big letters drawn on cardboard
scissors
glue
magazines
paper

What to do:

Method one
1 Cut shapes, colours, patterns and so on from a magazine.
2 Use these to embellish your letters.
3 Make sure you have covered the letters completely.

Method two
1 Cut out letters from magazines.
2 Glue the letters onto a page to form the words you want.

This can also be used as a spelling activity.

Photo montage

What you need:

magazines
scissors
glue
paper

What to do:

Cut out different pictures from a magazine and combine them to create your own photos.

Try to use different objects as textures. For example, a picture of straw cut into the shape of hair would be great for a clown.

Magazine distortion

What you need:

magazines
pencils
ruler
paper
scissors
glue

What to do:

Method one
1 Cut a photograph from a magazine.
2 Divide it into equal strips on the back and number them.
3 Cut the picture into these strips.
4 Glue the strips down in order, placing an imaginary line between each strip by leaving a small space.
5 Trace around the outside of the picture and hang it.

Method two
1 Mark and rule the back of the page in equidistant verticle strips.
2 Draw two lines on the backing sheet, about 2 cm above and below the length of the picture.
3 Glue the strips on alternately from top to bottom in order.

Once the children have mastered this, why not try using two pictures of the same size by gluing a strip from each alternately.

Effective results can be obtained from other geometric shapes as well.

Magazine collage

What you need:

magazines
glue
scissors
paper to be used as a backing sheet

What to do:

1 Choose a theme for your collage.
2 Cut out anything from magazines relating to that theme.
3 Arrange these pieces on the backing sheet.
4 When you are satisfied with the design glue the pieces down.

Scene construction

What you need:

magazines
paper
glue
scissors

What to do:

1 Decide on the scene to be made.
2 Cut out magazine pictures that will give you the texture effect you want. For example, a picture of brown carpet would be great for a tree trunk.
3 Draw the shape you need onto these pictures and cut out the shape.
4 Paste your scene together.

Other uses for magazines

- Use the pictures to write from.

- Cut out different things to decorate home-made game boards, cards etc.

- Use pictures to help you draw. For example, trace the outlines of a picture you may want the children to work on onto an overhead transparency and project it up to the size you want it drawn. Use various art techniques to colour it in. Use this technique for bodies if you have trouble drawing people.

paper

Aim

To create a number of different art forms which will demonstrate the many uses of paper as an art medium.

General objectives

- ■ To gain skill in using scissors
- ■ To experience paper folding techniques
- ■ To appreciate the wide variety of uses for paper
- ■ To increase skill in scoring, cutting and folding of paper

Doodle art

What you need:

coloured squares
scissors
glue

What to do:

1 Choose a doodle shape you have drawn and three sheets of contrasting coloured paper.
2 Trace your design on to the first coloured sheet and cut it out.
3 Now lay this cut-out on to the next coloured sheet and trace around it about 1 cm away from the first one so the second, when cut out, is bigger than the first.
4 Using this bigger cut-out, place it on the final sheet and trace and cut it 1 cm larger again.
5 Glue the biggest one on to a backing sheet, position the middle one on top of this, centre it and glue it down. Now centre the smallest one on top and glue it in to position.
6 Now you can hang a three-dimensional picture.

Wet tissue paper

What you need:

torn tissue paper
paper
glue wash - 1 part glue, 3 parts water
newspaper

What to do:

1 Brush the glue mixture over the surface of your page.
2 Now lay your tissue down and paint all over it as well with the glue.
3 Continue this until your page is covered.

Personality silhouette

What you need:

paper
adhesive tape
scissors
magazines
glue
an overhead or slide projector

What to do:

1 Tape your paper to the wall.
2 Sit in a chair in front of this.
3 Shine the light source onto the paper.
4 Get someone to draw around your shape.
5 Now look through magazines for things that best reflect you! Cut them out.
6 Remember, these can be words, pictures, or anything at all.
7 Arrange these inside your silhouette until you are happy with the result and glue them down.
8 Cut out your silhouette and frame it.

Play on shadows

What you need:

1 sheet dark coloured construction paper
2 sheets plain paper (one to be used as a backing sheet)
glue
scissors
crayons

What to do:

1 Hold both pieces of paper together and cut out the shape you wish to use, eg, a tree or an animal.
2 Glue the plain paper shape on to a sheet of paper.
3 Now glue the darker one slightly overlapping with the first.
4 Put in the surrounding effects with your crayons.

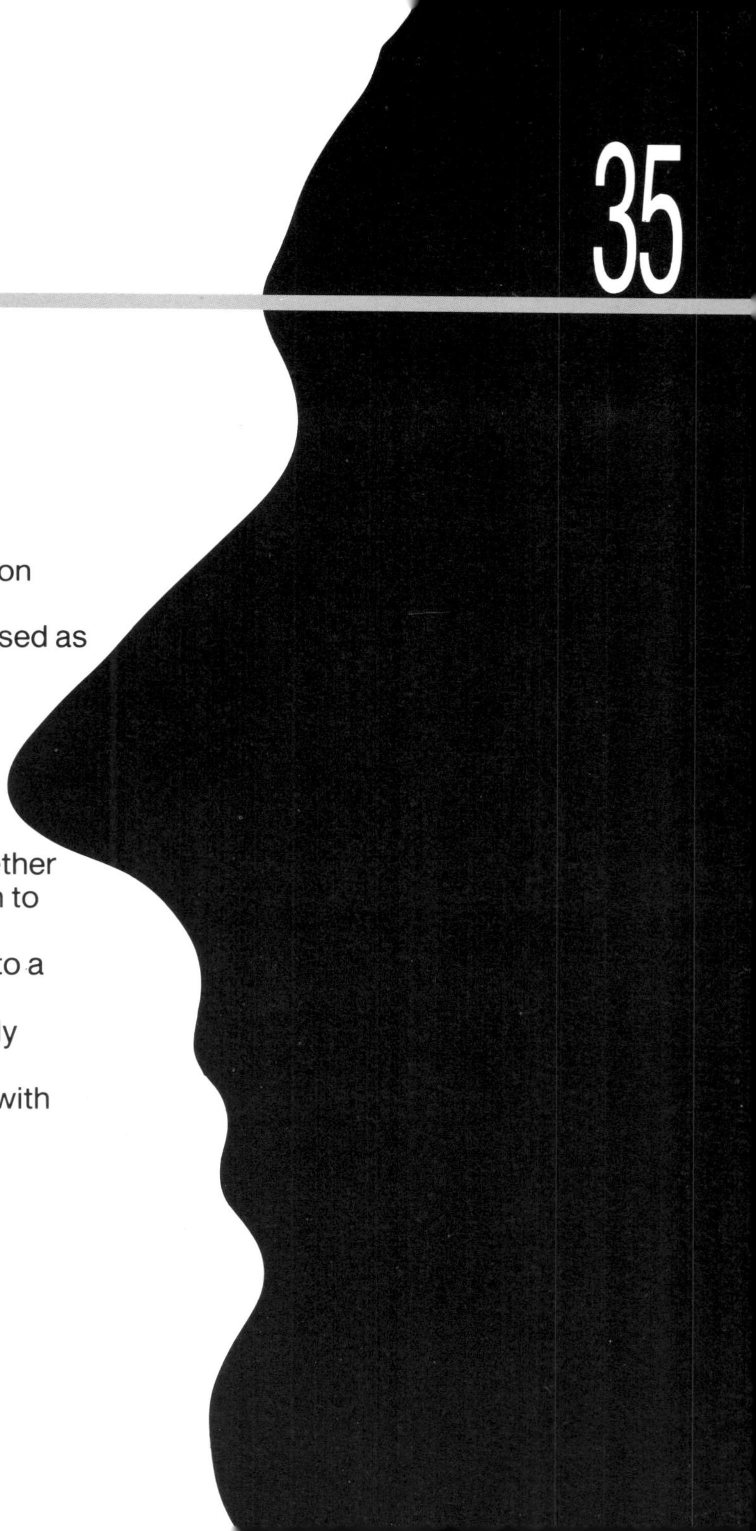

Negative positive designs

What you need:

coloured squares
plain paper
scissors
glue

What to do:

1 Fold a coloured square in half.
2 Cut a shape out of the coloured square by cutting into the fold - a light pencil drawing can make it easier.
3 Unfold the paper and glue it onto the plain sheet.
4 Unfold the shape you cut out and glue it beside the sheet you cut it from.

Geometric pictures

What you need:

coloured paper
glue
scissors

What to do:

1 Cut up a variety of different shapes in a variety of colours and sizes.

2 Play with these on your page until they make a picture of something - you may find you need to cut more of a particular shape once you start working.
3 When you are satisfied with the arrangement glue it down.

Cut paper patterns

What you need:

coloured backing paper
plain white paper
scissors

What to do:

1 Fold the blank page in half and then in half again. Now fold it diagonally to make a triangle.
2 Cut patterns into the edges of the shape.
3 Open this up and mount it on some brightly coloured paper.

You can also fold the paper into eights and cut away to create a more intricate pattern.

Window decorations

What you need:

white tissue paper
brightly coloured inks
brushes
newspaper
scissors
black paper squares

What to do:

1 Lay the tissue paper on some newspaper.
2 Using a thick brush and ink or thick poster paint, dab on lots of bright colours until you have covered the page.
3 Hang this to dry.
4 While you wait for the tissue paper to dry, cut out your frame by folding the black paper in half and half again, then diagonally to make a triangle.
5 Cut patterns out of the folded paper, making sure to leave a bit of each fold uncut - this will keep it together.
6 Unfold this and glue it to the tissue paper around the edges.
7 Trim the excess tissue paper off and hang it on your window.

Shadow pictures

What you need:

an action photo from a magazine
scissors
coloured paper

What to do:

1 Trace the outline of your figure onto light paper.
2 Attach this to a coloured square with a bit of Blu-Tac.
3 Put the other two sheets of coloured paper behind this so that when you cut it out you will have cut three at once.
4 Glue the figures onto a white page, slightly overlapping so that they look as though they are moving.
5 You can add other cut-outs to this to make it more complete, eg a soccer ball for a soccer player.

String up creations

What you need:

paper
pencils
scissors
glue

What to do:

1 Fold a long strip of paper into as many equal sections as you like.
2 On the top fold you can draw your design, making sure that the picture touches both folded sides in at least one place.
3 Cut out your design, unfold it and mount it if you wish.

Reflection pictures

What you need:

coloured paper
plain paper
pencils
scissors

What to do:

1 Fold your paper in half lengthways.
2 Write your name in thick letters, making sure that the base of each letter touches the fold or do a scene, making sure the base of it is on the fold also.
3 Cut out around your letters or design.
4 Open the page and glue it to a contrasting colour.

Nature paper

What you need:

tissues
wax paper
glue
water
sponge or brush
leaves, petals etc to be used as a pattern

What to do:

1 Tape some wax paper to your table.
2 Arrange your petals, leaves etc in a pattern on the wax paper.
3 Separate the tissue into a single thickness and lay it over your arrangement.
4 Mix 1 part glue and 3 parts water in a jar.
5 Dab this mixture all over the tissue and allow it to dry.
6 Trim and frame your paper.

Tissue paper flowers

What you need:

6 sheets tissue paper cut into a rectangle 26 cm x 37 cm
1 rubber band
1 pipe cleaner or twig

What to do:

1 Place the six sheets in an even pile.
2 Fold them into 2 cm pleats, as you would for a fan.
3 Place the rubber band in the centre of the pleated tissue and secure it tightly.
4 Gently pull up the first layer of tissue towards the rubber band.
5 Continue in this manner until all the sheets are up.
6 Fluff them slightly and you are ready to make the stem.
7 Slide a pipe cleaner through the rubber band and bend it over to secure it.
8 Twigs look very real when used as stems but just about anything can be used.

Paper wallets

What you need:

a piece of wrapping paper 30 cm x 50 cm
scissors
glue

What to do:

1 Making sure that the white side is facing you, fold the paper in half, lengthwise, and unfold it.
2 Fold the two top corners into the centre fold that you just made.
3 Bring the bottom of the page right up to the very top point and press down.
4 Bring the outer edges into the centre and fold them down.
5 Draw a line across the width of this, a third of the way from the top.
6 Fold the bottom edge up to meet this line.
7 Tuck the flap into the pocket and you have a wallet.

You can glue fabric on to firmer paper for a more durable wallet.

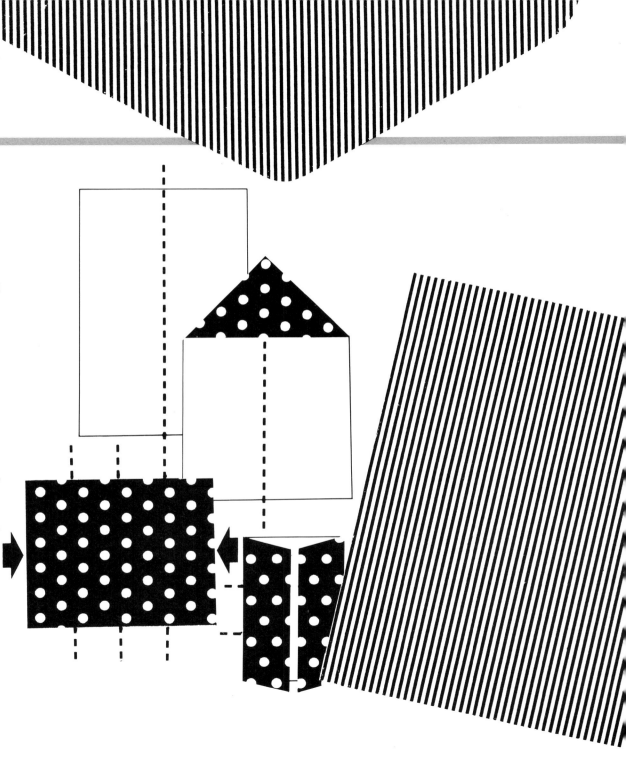

who said weaving's too hard?

Aim

To take the child through a number of graduated weaving activities which will foster the relevant skills involved in producing a piece of weaving.

General objectives

- To experience basic weaving activities which will enable the child to work with wool with a degree of expertise
- To become competent in the process of weaving
- To develop a comprehension of all weaving terms
- To feel satisfaction and enjoyment in the making of an article

The first activity for this unit is weaving paper. See page 29 for instructions.

Drinking straw weaving

What you need:

knitting yarn
drinking straws

What to do:

1 Cut five long, equal lengths of yarn.
2 Thread these through five straws.
3 Once threaded, knot these individually at the top of each straw so that all straws are equal and cannot slide off.
4 Gather the threads and knot them all together at the top and bottom of the straws.
5 Take a very long length of yarn and begin weaving over and under the straws.
6 When you have done about half the length of the straw you can undo the knots at the bottom and slide the straws down so that you can see your work.

This is a very easy way to start children in weaving yarns and you can have as many or as few straws as you like. You can also continue for as long as you like; just keep moving the straws.

More ideas for beginners

Weave on a fork for practice.

Weave on a shoe-box lid

Cut equidistant notches at the top and bottom of the lid. Now wind the wool up and down on to these. Once you have done this and they are secured, you can start weaving across.

Weave on a margarine lid

Cut a small hole in the centre of a margarine or ice-cream lid. Now make an odd number of equidistant notches around the edge of the lid. Thread this so that you create something that looks like a wheel with spokes. When this is done, start weaving in a circular motion from the centre out.

Mexican gods-eyes

What you need:

yarns of various colours (two is sufficient)
twigs, rulers or sticks

What to do:

1 Try to get two sticks that are roughly the same length.
2 Join these together in the centre with string or glue.
3 Attach your first colour to the centre and push the knot to the back.
4 Start to wind by going over and around the first arm, then over and around the next one and so on until you are ready to change colours.
5 Change colours by attaching the yarn at the back so the knot does not show.

Pot holders

What you need:

a square of firm cardboard
two different coloured wools

What to do:

1 Cut an odd number of equidistant notches in the top and bottom of the cardboard.
2 Wind the wool up and down through the notches.
3 Start weaving across, stopping occasionally to push the wool tightly towards the top.
4 When you have reached the bottom, make sure it is firm and knot the end in.
5 Now turn your cardboard over and cut the threads at the back in the middle of the cardboard.
6 Knot these firmly at each end so your weaving does not slip off.
7 These ends can be trimmed, frayed for fringing or threaded in the back of your pot holder.

Nature weaving

What you need:

twigs, long reeds, grasses, string, wool, beads, weeds and anything you think will look good
firm cardboard or masonite for the backing

What to do:

1 Notch the cardboard or masonite the same way as potholder weaving.
2 Roll a newspaper up and put it horizontally behind the board so that you wind the loom up over the paper - this will give the warp threads enough slack to accommodate twigs and rods etc.
3 Weave a firm twig or rod along the top and bottom for the frame.
4 Now you can weave through just about anything to create a beautiful wall hanging.

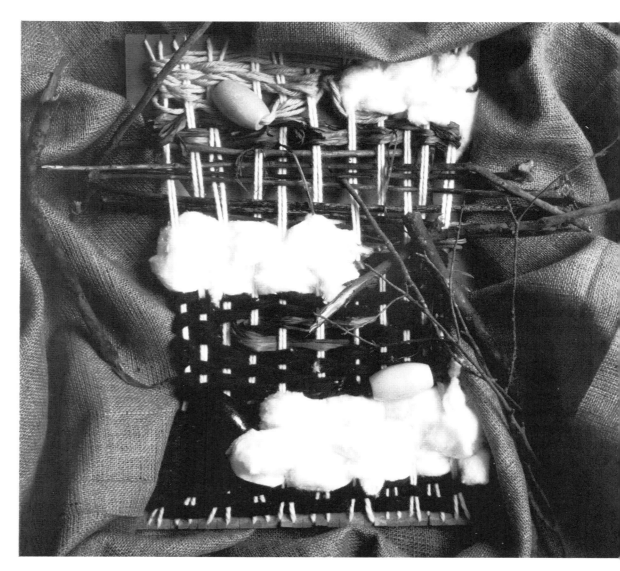

expressing
feeling
through
colour

Aim

To involve the child in colour as a means
for expression of mood and feeling.

General objectives

■ To discover that certain colours can
convey warmth and coldness
■ To be able to display colours in contrast
through various art media
■ To experience the depth of colour
through thinning with water
■ To experience the blending of two
colours in an effort to create a new one
■ To gain experience in using colour as a
vehicle for expression of feeling

Cool colour

What you need:

torn tissue paper in cool colours
glue wash (2 parts water 1 part glue)
paper
brushes
cool colour pictures for discussion

What to do:

1 Discuss the colours which convey a cool feeling.
2 Now cover your page with the glue wash.
3 Place pieces of tissue paper on your page and cover them with glue wash.
4 Continue doing this until the page is covered in cool coloured paper.

Warm colour

What you need:

magazines
paper
scissors
glue
warm colour pictures for discussion

What to do:

1 Study magazine pictures which display only warm colours, eg sunsets - orange, yellow, red etc.
2 Cut out parts of magazine photographs which convey warmth.
3 Arrange these on your page and glue them down to create your own warm collage.

Contrast designs

What you need:

examples from the previous two lessons
coloured squares of contrasting colour
scissors
pencil

What to do:

1 Discuss the colours which convey warm and cool feelings.
2 Choose two squares of contrasting colour.
3 Fold one square in half - cut this and keep one half aside (this will not be used).
4 Fold the smaller half again and draw a simple design along the fold.
5 Cut this out and open both pieces.
6 Glue both these pieces onto the contrasting square.

Make sure that you leave the top and bottom of the fold uncut.

Intensity paint washes

What you need:

paint
plenty of water
brushes
black paint

What to do:

1 Start at the top of your page and paint a 3 cm wide strip in pure paint straight from the tube.
2 Immediately dip the brush into water and paint another band of colour.
3 Repeat this until you have reached the bottom of your page.
4 Once it is dry, use the black paint to draw a silhouette over it to complete the picture.

Making colours with blob prints

What you need:

paint
paper
pens

What to do:

1 Fold your page in half and open it again.
2 Place blobs of colour on the fold beside each other.
3 Be sure to give the child only colours that will create new ones, eg blue, yellow, red to obtain green, orange and purple.
4 Open your page and see if you can work out what colours you made and by using what colours.
5 Discuss why the pattern is mirrored.

descriptive and expressive 48

line

Aim

To investigate the properties of line as an element of design.

General objectives

■ To explore both the descriptive and expressive ways in which line can be used

■ To investigate the visual properties of line

■ To utilise line to communicate feeling

The first activity in this unit deals with line distortion. See magazine distortion page 31 for instructions.

Expressive line

What you need:

a variety of writing implements
paper

What to do:

1 Discuss the different ways that you
can represent line, eg straight,
curved, heavy, light, thick, thin, sharp,
smooth, shaky, strong, definite etc.
2 Try to represent these on paper using
different implements.

Exploring descriptive line

What you need:

fruit and vegetables, cut in half
pencils, pens or felt pens

What to do:

1 Study the patterns in the fruit or
vegetable that you have dissected.
2 Put the fruit or vegetable down onto
your paper and trace around it.
3 Try to reproduce all of the lines found
inside the fruit.

Hand decorations

What you need:

your hands
felt pen

What to do:

1 Lay your hands on the paper with your fingers spread out and trace around them.
2 Embellish the background using the various types of line you used in the previous exercise.
3 Draw a thick black line around the page and hang it up.

Try tracing nature.

Using continuous line

What you need:

PVA glue
paper
pencils
ink or paint wash

What to do:

1 Draw a continuous line on your page with a pencil.
2 Trace over this with PVA glue and allow to dry.
3 Cover the page with ink or paint wash.
4 The glue will resist the ink to expose a white line pattern.

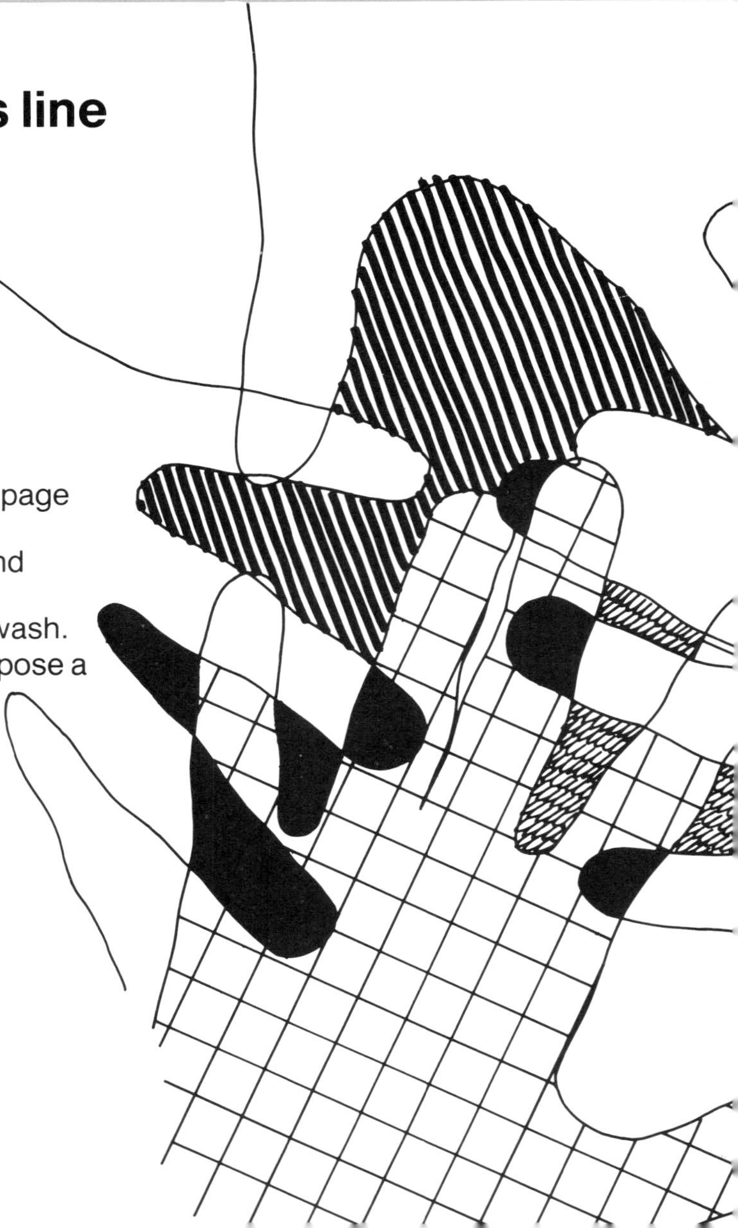

A line box study

What you need:

a simple drawing
paper
ruler
felt pens

What to do:

1 Cut your drawing up into six equal
   boxes.
2 Rearrange the boxes on another
   sheet so that the page has been put
   back together but is mixed up.
3 Secure these in position and lay a
   blank sheet over the page.
4 Trace your mixed-up page onto the
   blank sheet.
5 Using all the skills in line that you have
   experienced, embellish the picture.

puppetry

Aim

Through the making of various puppets, children will be able to experience design, modelling, costume creating and construction skills which are all essential art practices.

General objectives

■ To gain skill in the construction of puppets
■ To become familiar with various glues and joining techniques
■ To develop self confidence through the use of finished puppets in language activities.
■ To develop modelling skills through papier mâché techniques.

Objectives which spring into other curriculum areas:

■ To utilise the puppets made as a tool for improving communication skills
■ To further develop drama skills
■ To give opportunities for play writing and acting

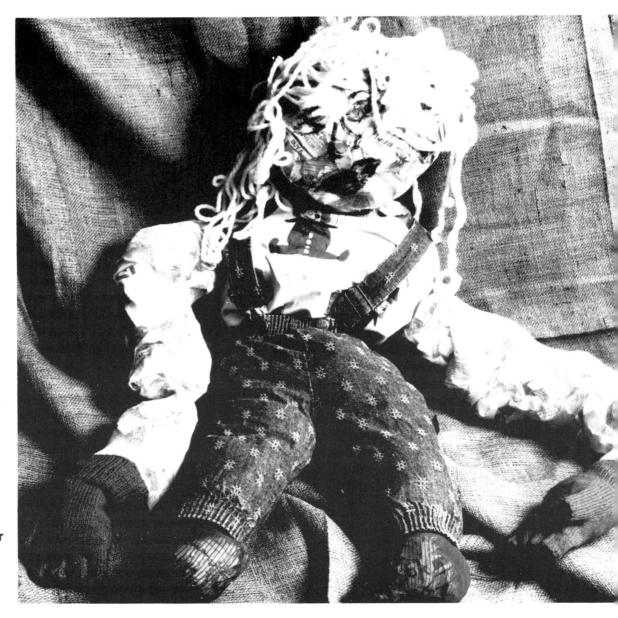

Free construction puppets

What you need:

brown paper bags
boxes
foam
paper cups
egg cartons
paddlepop sticks
paper (a wide variety)
old wooden spoons
wool scraps
cloth scraps
pipe cleaners
pins
paste
adhesive tape
staplers
buttons
ribbons
any odds and ends for decoration

What to do:

1 Allow the children to select, organise and reorganise materials until they make a decision regarding the type of puppets to be made. Discuss facial features, moving limbs if any, hair, how to hold the puppet and so on.

2 Construct the puppets to suit your whim, exploring all mediums available as well as suitable joining techniques.

Basic hand puppets

What you need:

coloured construction paper
glue
scissors

What to do:

1 Fold the paper in half and then fold each edge back towards the fold.
2 The fold then becomes a mouth which you can open and close by placing your hand in the open ends.
3 Embellish your puppet as desired, adding eyes, teeth, tongue etc.

Finger puppets

What you need:

old wool scraps
fabric remnants
rubber gloves
construction paper
felt pieces
buttons
cotton wool
glitter
odds and ends for decoration

What to do:

1 Draw on paper the shape of your puppets making sure it will go around your finger if you are not using rubber gloves as a basis to work from.
2 Pin the drawing onto the main material to be used and cut it out.
3 Join the sides together to make the finger tube and embellish to make the puppet of your choice.

Jack-in-the-box

What you need:

margarine containers
paddlepop stick or ruler
socks
elastic bands
paper
odds and ends for decoration

What to do:

1 Make a head for your puppet by screwing paper up into a tight ball and attaching it to your stick.
2 Make a small opening in the base of your container and slide the stick through.
3 Cover the head and margarine container with a sock decorated as the type of puppet you wish.
4 When you want the puppet to disappear into the container simply pull the stick down.

Papier mâché puppetry

What you need:

papier mâché (see recipe file, page 89)
shape to mâché over, eg small balloon,
styrofoam ball, light bulb etc
cardboard cylinder
decorative scraps

What to do:

1 Attach the shape to mâché over to the
  tube and stand the tube in plasticine
  or attach to the desk so that you have
  a steady base to work on.
2 Cover the head and top of the tube
  with papier mâché building up
  features as you go.
3 Allow your work to dry for a few days
  before painting it.
4 Add clothing, hair and other features
  to your construction.

Dough/clay marionettes

What you need:

dough or clay (see recipe file, page 89)
paddlepop sticks
string
paint
decorative materials
knitting needle or similar implement

What to do:

1 Using the dough, model your puppet
  in separate body pieces.
2 Use a knitting needle or similar
  implement to insert holes through the
  limbs to thread the string through.
3 Insert holes to attach the body to the
  limbs.
4 If using dough, bake at the required
  temperature before threading
  together and painting.

5 Decorate your puppet by adding
  clothes, features, hair and so on.
6 Join two paddlepop sticks in the
  centre to form a cross and attach a
  length of string at each of the four ends.
7 Now attach the end of these strings to
  the limbs so that you can move them.

Another simple marionette is the
stuffed sack or stocking puppet which
is filled with crushed newspaper and
joined loosely with string.

Aim

To provide valuable tactile experiences which will allow children to manipulate and acquire skill in three-dimensional materials.

General objectives

- To gain hand-building skills through pinch and coil construction
- To experience the properties of clay and demonstrate skill in the manipulation of it
- To develop an understanding of the relevant vocabulary associated with clay work
- To experiment with a wide variety of materials in an effort to produce interesting textures and surfaces
- To feel pride and satisfaction in the making of clay objects

Vocabulary associated with clay

Bisque: unglazed pottery which has been fired once.

Greenware: clay which has dried out thoroughly and ready for firing.

Joining: process used to join up pieces of clay by moistening both pieces with water and pressing firmly together. Rub with fingers to smooth the join.

Wedge: process used to remove any air bubbles from the clay by slamming, pushing, pressing and doubling over as you would when kneading bread dough.

Throwing: a process of shaping clay on a rotating wheel.

Other words the children may use: squeeze, push, fire, glaze, coil, pebble, roll, punch, kiln, texture, slab pinch, knead, sieve, hollow out, press and slip.

Important facts to remember

- Clay should be stored in airtight containers or bags.
- Clay should be kept moist. Clay which is left over should be stored with a sponge in the bottom of the bag to soak up excess water. A hole can be made in the clay with your thumb and filled with water before sealing the bag.
- Clay will dry out if it is exposed to air for too long.
- Disinfectant may be added to leftover clay in the water hole; this will keep it fresh.
- All air bubbles must be removed from clay before sculpting, as the object may burst during firing if bubbles remain.
- Do not make the clay too wet as it will stick to your hands like a soggy cake mixture.
- If the clay becomes hard and unmanagable, sprinkle with water, wet your hands and work it in.
- If you are making a pot, tap it gently on the table and this will give a flat base.
- When leaving sculptured clay to dry out, sit it on either newspaper or paper towel as this will shrink with the clay and not distort it.
- Clay needs to be dried slowly at room temperature and out of the sun. If it is a very hot day lay a damp cloth over the individual pieces.

Please refer to recipe file, page 90, for clay substitute recipes, ie dough, salt ceramics, play dough etc.

Hand-building skills

What you need:

clay
water
surface to work on
drying space
glaze (optional)

What to do:

Pinch pot

1 Take a ball of clay about the size of your fist and wedge thoroughly to remove air bubbles.
2 Roll the clay into a smooth round ball.
3 Push your thumb into the centre of the ball and start working from the centre out with thumb and index finger. Keep turning the pot as you go for even thickness.
4 When you are satisfied with the shape of your pot, tap it gently on the bottom to give it a flat base.
5 You can embellish the pot with patterns or textures before leaving to dry for firing and glazing.

Coil pot

1 Take a ball of clay the size of your fist and wedge thoroughly.
2 Roll the clay into long strips just as you would when making snakes.
3 Flatten a piece of clay and cut out a shape to be the base.
4 Build up the coils on top of the base to the required height.
5 The pot can be smoothed on the inside.

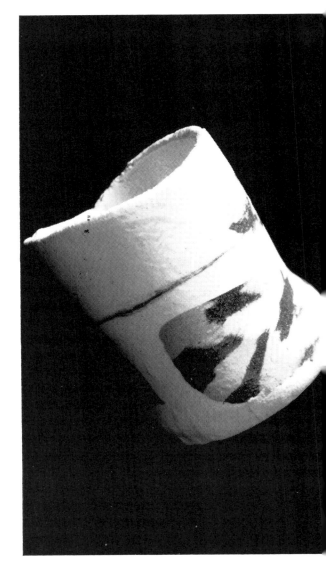

Animal and object making

The following is a list of utensils which may be used in order to explore and create with texture and pattern.

What you need:

sticks
nails
shells
bottle tops
pencils
hessian
drinking straws
beads
buttons
toothpicks
wire
string
leaves
kitchen utensils
coffee grains, sawdust etc can give an interesting texture and will fire out.

All children should experience squeezing clay through a garlic press to make hair or whatever.

What to do:

1 Wedge the clay to remove air bubbles.

2 Allow the child to explore the clay - to roll, pull, twist squeeze and so on.
3 Using a variety of media, develop an animal or object which has interesting patterns and textures.

Moulded pots

What you need:

clay
plastic moulds, eg ice-cream buckets,
margarine containers etc
hessian or old sheeting

What to do:

1 Lay the fabric inside the plastic
   container to be used so that you can
   easily remove your work when
   finished.
2 Divide your clay up into small balls
   about the size of ping pong balls.
3 Press these balls into the side of the
   container and the base until you have
   made a pot to the size you want.
4 A combination of coil, slab and pebble
   methods may be used .
5 When you have finished the pot, use
   your fingers to smooth the inside to
   ensure all pieces are joined and no
   cracks are present.
6 Allow to harden at room temperature
   before removing from the mould and
   firing.

Leaf print dishes

What you need:

leaves with definite veins or textures,
eg ferns, jacaranda or maple
clay
rolling pins
cardboard bowls (paper plate type)
implement to cut the clay, eg bamboo
skewers

What to do:

1 Take a piece of clay the size of your
   fist and wedge well to remove air
   bubbles.
2 Roll this out with a rolling pin to
   approximately 0.25 cm thick.
3 Carefully lay the leaf down on this
   slab and roll it gently to press in the
   print of the leaf.
4 Peel the leaf up carefully to expose
   the print.
5 Lay in a cardboard bowl to form the
   dish shape and allow to dry out for
   firing.

Tea bag holders

What you need:

clay
textures, eg hessian, mesh etc
cutting implement, eg bamboo skewer
newspaper

What to do:

1 Take a piece of clay about the size of a grapefruit and wedge thoroughly.
2 Halve the ball and flatten the halves out with your hands to about 0.5 cm thick.
3 Cut out the size you wish to have as the back of the sack and cut roughly the same size for the front.
4 If adding a texture to the front, eg hessian print, press this in firmly to the front.
5 Roll some newspaper up into a ball and place this on the back slab.
6 Gently lay the front over this and pinch the edges together with your fingers all around, leaving the opening at the top.
7 The newspaper will keep the bag in shape and open while drying occurs.
8 Gently tap the bag onto the table to make a flat base which will enable the holder to stand on its own.

Flower holders

What you need:

clay
newspaper
cutting implement
textures if desired

What to do:

1 Flatten out your wedged clay into a large oval shape approximately 25 cm long.
2 Fold this in half and cut through the fold so that you have two pieces on top of each other.
3 Add texture to the surface of your top layer.
4 Fill the inside with crushed newspaper to make the opening.
5 Pinch the edges together and place a hole for the string.

Doll mobiles

What you need:

clay
leather thonging
string or yarn
knitting needles or bamboo skewers

What to do:

1 Wedge the clay to be used.
2 Shape the body parts by rolling tubes
  of clay and, using a knitting needle,
  put a hole at each end for the string.
  Make sure that the hole is large
  enough for the string.
3 Allow the clay to dry and be fired
  before threading your body together.

easy
expressive
64

sculpture

Aim

To utilise a wide range of art media in an individual way to make a pleasing sculpture.

Objectives

■ To gain skill in the manipulation of unusual art media
■ To further extend aesthetic sense through the arranging and rearranging of objects.
■ To acquire social skills necessary for the completion of a piece of art work which is the product of group effort.

Pea and toothpick mobiles

What you need:

toothpicks
food colourings
shelled peas

What to do:

1 Soak the toothpicks overnight in different food colourings so that you have a variety of coloured toothpicks to work from.
2 Shell the peas when you are ready to use them.
3 Put a pea at each end of the toothpick.
4 Put other toothpicks into these peas, adding more peas and toothpicks as you go.
5 Continue in this manner until you have an interesting sculpture.
6 Leave this a few days for the peas to dry out and shrivel.
7 Attach a piece of string and hang.
8 Try not to put too many picks into the one pea as it will split. You can also do this with marshmallows but you'll have to eat them when you've finished.

Drinking straw sculpture

What you need:

different coloured drinking straws
PVA glue
scissors
cardboard

What to do:

1 Cut the straws to varying lengths ranging from 1 cm to approximately 2 cm.
2 Draw the picture or shape to be sculptured on the cardboard.
3 Use the glue to secure your straws to the board.
4 When finished, leave your work on a flat surface to dry.

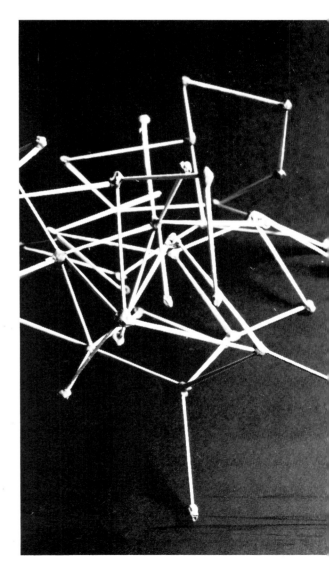

Group work junk sculptures

What you need:

Anything you can collect which you
think you can use, eg toilet rolls, boxes,
scrap material and so on.
PVA glue
cardboard

What to do:

1 In your group, decide what you will
   aim to make. You might start with one
   idea and end up with something
   totally different.
2 When satisfied with the product,
   spray paint or decorate it.

Squashy sculptures

What you need:

plaster of Paris
water
plastic bags
string
fine sandpaper
paint

What to do:

1 Mix the plaster to a creamy consistency.
2 Pour it into the plastic bag and tie it with string.
3 When the plaster starts to harden and become thick, squeeze the bag with both hands and hold it until the plaster sets (it helps if you are in the sun).
4 When it is firm, use the sandpaper to create whatever shape you like. Now you can paint it.

Wrapped wire sculpture

What you need:

thin wire
plaster of Paris bandages
water
heavy card

What to do:

1 Bend and model the wire into the form of a body or an unusual shape.
2 Secure the wire sculpture at the base to a board with tape so you can work on it.
3 Cut the plaster bandages into strips, dip into the water and begin wrapping around the wire.
4 Continue building up your sculpture in this manner until you are satisfied.

simple
ways
with

jewellery

making

Aim

To investigate jewellery making as a
craft with a wide range of media.

Objectives
■ To acquire skill in basic enamelling
■ To explore modelling techniques
through materials such as dough, Fimo
clay etc
■ To experience a sense of pride and joy
in the completion of a series of
individually crafted jewellery samples

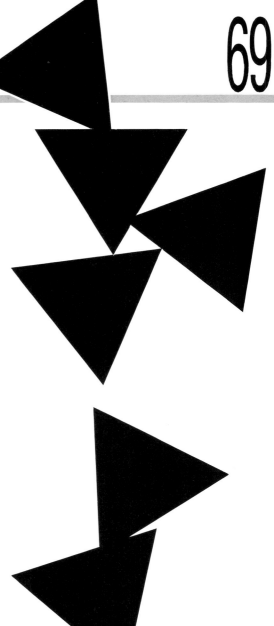

Modelling dough beads and things

What you need:

jewellery dough (see recipe file, page 89)
toothpicks
paint

What to do:

1 Roll a variety of shapes to be used as beads.
2 Pierce each bead with the toothpick.
3 Allow the beads to dry and harden.
4 Paint if desired and string up.
5 These beads may be coated with lacquer or clear nail polish to make the colour brighter and the bead more durable.

Paper jewellery

What you need:

coloured paper squares
PVA glue
sandpaper
lacquer or clear nail polish
jewellery backings if needed, eg brooch or earring

What to do:

1 Draw a shape which is easy to repeat and cut out about twenty from the coloured squares.
2 Glue these together, one on top of the other.
3 Wait until they are completely dry before sanding around the edges to make a more interesting shape.
4 Coat with lacquer or nail polish.

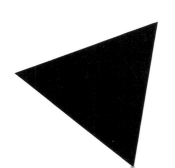

Plaster bandage jewellery

What you need:

plaster of Paris bandages
bottles, thick pens and any other shape
to model on
water
wax paper
scissors
paint
adhesive tape

What to do:

1 Choose a cylindrical shape which is the right size for the jewellery you wish to make.
2 Wrap a piece of wax paper around the area you will be modelling and secure it with tape.
3 Cut the plaster bandages into strips and wrap these around the shape.
4 Continue in this manner until your jewellery is the thickness required.
5 When dry, remove it from the mould and use the sandpaper to smooth the surface ready for decoration.

Copper enamelled jewellery

What you need:

small copper shapes and accessories
(these can be obtained through
government stores or art suppliers)
low bake enamel (also available from
government stores and art suppliers)
steel wool
candles
plasticine
flat blunt knives

What to do:

1 Clean the copper piece to be enamelled with steel wool.
2 Sprinkle a little enamel powder evenly onto the piece.
3 Push the candle into the plasticine so that it stands alone, and light it.
4 Using the knife, slide your piece up and hold it about 3 cm above the flame.
5 Watch the powder melt into a paint. When all the powder has changed the piece is done (approximately thirty seconds).
6 Allow to cool.

Fimo modelling dough

What you need:

Fimo modelling dough (available from
art suppliers)
jewellery backings if needed, eg brooch
or earring
oven

What to do:

1 Cut a small piece from each of the
  various colours and work them like
  bread dough until manageable.
2 Model these into whatever shapes
  you like.
3 Bake on a cookie tin at the required
  temperature for approximately 10 to
  15 minutes.

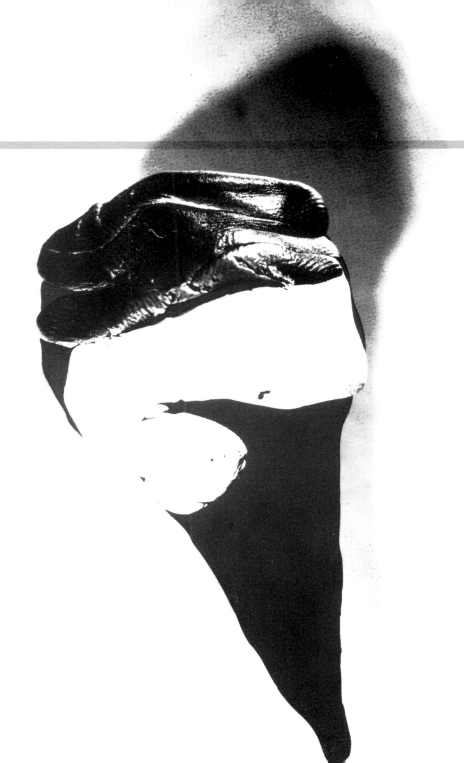

batik
for
beginners

Aim

To provide children with a series of
activities enabling them to become
proficent in the batik process.

Objectives

■ For the child to become familiar with the
various tools involved in batik
■ To develop competence in making
unusual and effective samples of batik
■ To acquire understanding in the 'wax
resist' principle

Paper batik

What you need:

wax of any kind, eg crayon, candle etc
paper
brushes
paint or dye

What to do:

1 Cover the page as best you can with wax.
2 Crinkle the page tightly into a ball (thus cracking the wax).
3 Gently unfold and lie flat but do not press.
4 Paint the entire page with a watery paint.
5 If the effect is not sufficient give the paper another careful crumple while wet.

Substitute paste batik

What you need:

paste (see recipe file, page 89)
instruments to apply the paste
material scraps, eg old T-shirts etc
brushes and sponges

What to do:

1 Apply the paste in desired manner directly onto the material.
2 Leave this overnight to dry.
3 When dry, crinkle the material and roll it into a ball in order to crack the paste.
4 Lay the material out flat and paint the dye straight on.
5 Once the dye is dry you can either scrape or soak the paste off depending on the type of dye used.

Batik wax eggs

What you need:

eggs
dye bath
wax or crayons
toothpicks
needle

What to do:

1 To blow out the egg pierce a hole at either end. Blow through the smaller hole. An egg kept at room temperature is easier to blow.
2 Apply the wax with a crayon or melted wax with a toothpick.
3 Dip the eggs into the dye bath.
4 Allow to dry before removing the wax.
5 Wax can be removed by placing the egg in a 250 degree oven until the wax becomes shiny. Wipe clean with a cloth.

Material batik

What you need:

material
wax parrafin and bees' wax
double boilers or frying pans
paint brushes
dye baths
iron
paper

What to do:

1 Melt the wax in a double boiler.
2 Paint the wax onto the material where dye is not required.
3 When the wax has cooled and hardened crinkle the material into a ball in order to crack the wax.
4 Either dip the material into a dye bath or apply different colours with a brush.
5 When dry, either scrape the wax off or iron the fabric between two sheets of towelling to soak up the wax.

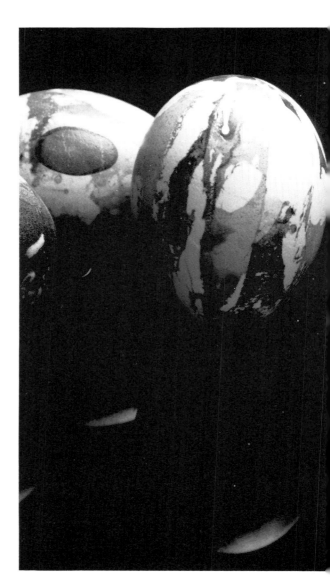

tie-dye techniques

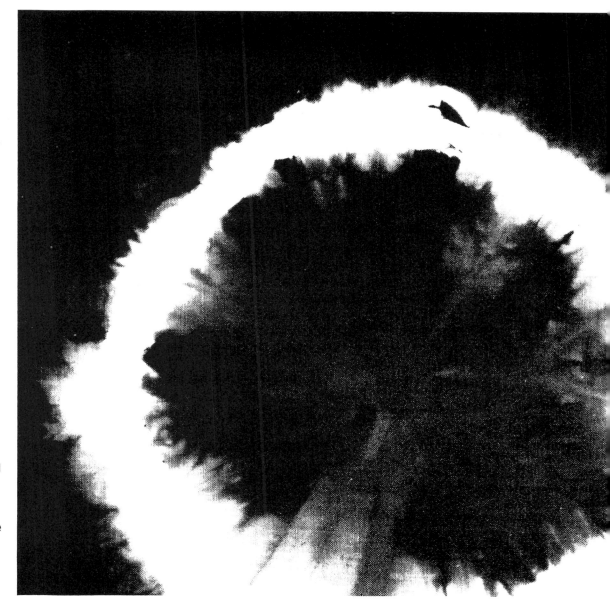

Aim

To explore the resist technique with fabrics through a variety of graded tie-dye methods.

General objectives

■ To develop skill and proficency in doing a number of tie-dye knots
■ To gain experience in resist techniques through the dyeing process
■ To acquire skill in making and using dye baths which will give several colours to one cloth
■ To become familiar with the various tie-dye terms involved in the process

Peg dyeing

What you need:

clothes pegs or bulldog clips
fabric
dye bath (see recipe file, page 89, for homemade vegetable dyes)

What to do:

1 Wet the cloth to be dyed in cold water and squeeze it out.
2 Fold the material in the pattern desired.
3 Secure pegs or bulldog clips around the fabric.
4 Immerse the entire work in the dye and leave for approximately 20 minutes.
5 Remove and rinse in cold water.

Dip and dye fabrics

What you need:

dye containers
fabric dye
squares of scrap fabric

What to do:

1 Fold the sheet of fabric in an interesting manner until it is reasonably small.
2 To save mess you can secure a peg to the fabric to act as a holder.
3 Dip each corner into different coloured dyes and hold for 5 to 10 minutes.
4 Open the fabric out and iron when dry.

A hot dye bath is often better for this technique.

Crayon resist tie-dye

What you need:

brightly coloured crayons
scrap fabric
dye baths
string or rubber bands

What to do:

1 Draw a design with crayons directly onto the fabric, making sure that you press firmly.
2 Tie the fabric into bunches with either rubber bands or string.
3 Dip into the dye.
4 Remove ties and hang to dry.

Stick tie-dyeing

What you need:

cloth
dye baths
sticks
string or elastic bands

What to do:

1 Wet your material and lay it out open on the table.
2 Stand your stick in the centre and wrap the material up around the stick.
3 Secure your fabric to the stick by wrapping rubber bands or string around it from the top to the bottom.
4 Immerse one end of the sitck in one colour for the required time and then remove and immerse the other end in a different coloured dye bath.

Multicoloured tie-dyeing

What you need:

cloth
dye baths
string or rubber bands

What to do:

1 Wet your material in cold water and squeeze out the excess.
2 Tie only a few sections of the material and immerse into one colour.
3 Take out and rinse but do not take the rubber bands off.
4 Add a few more ties to your fabric and immerse in another colour.
5 Rinse and add more ties if you wish to immerse into a third colour.
6 Rinse thoroughly and remove all ties.

Bleach tie-dyes

What you need:

bleach bath
coloured fabric (old blue jeans are great
as well as black fabrics and cottons)
elastic bands

What to do:

1 Wet the fabric with cold water and
  squeeze out the excess water.
2 Tie tightly with elastic bands.
3 Dip the tied sections into the bleach
  for approximately 5 minutes and
  remove.
4 Rinse out and remove the bands to
  expose your design.

Some knots to get into a tangle over

Doughnut knot

Gather up a section of material and
push the top through the centre and
down through your hands.
Bind with elastic at the base.

Rosette knot

Pinch up a section of the cloth and tie at
the base. You can add bands on top of
the base band leading up to the top of
the bunch which will give you circular
patterns within each other.

Fold

Gather and/or pleat the material all the
way to the end and tie bands in any
pattern.

The twist

Twist the cloth as tightly as you can
from beginning to end and tie the ends
together. You can either immerse it in
the dye as is or you can tie with bands
as well.

Rubber bands

Thick rubber bands give larger designs
while thin bands will give a thin spidery
effect. The same applies to the types of
string you use. It is important to try and
wrap the string on top of itself a few
times to ensure dye does not leak in
underneath.

solving

drawing

79

dilemmas

Aim

To experience a variety of drawing techniques in order to improve overall drawing skill.

General objectives

- To experience observation drawing techniques
- To further develop memory drawing skills
- To become familiar with basic perspective techniques
- To gain practice in mediated drawing techniques

Some simple types of drawing styles

Memory drawing

Drawing from memory images of either an experience or an object. This type of drawing is often called recall drawing.

Direct observation drawing

Careful, critical observation of objects, scenes, people and so on recorded on paper, eg still life drawing.

Imaginary drawing

Building or extrapolating on recall objects to make new or unusual images - creating with the mind and pencil, eg drawing a view of a garden from an ant's eyes.

Mediated drawing

Using art forms whether they be famous works of art or your own and creating a new impression of them, eg copying a sketch using painting or collage techniques.

Observational drawing

What you need:

paper
drawing implement
board (optional)
object to draw

What to do:

1 Set up the object to be drawn.
2 Make sure everybody has a view.
3 Attach the page to the board in a way
   which corresponds with what you are
   drawing, eg something big requires a
   vertical position.
4 If working from a drawing board hold
   it at a slight angle.
5 Set a time limit.
6 Talk briefly on everything to be seen.
7 Try not to rub out but to correct from
   your first lines.
8 Stress the need for silence.
9 Never move from your chair as this
   will change the angle and view point
   you have.
10 Date your work, border it with a
   black felt-tipped pen and file it.

This task can sometimes only take 5 to
10 minutes and when done frequently
you will see a vast improvement in drawing.

Memory drawing

What you need:

your memory
last night's dinner
drawing implements
paper

What to do:

1 Arrange your paper so that you can pretend it is a placemat.
2 Draw on the placemat the cutlery and dishes, plates and so on that you used for last night's dinner in the same position on the mat.
3 Add to this either the food that you had last night or perhaps your favourite food.
4 Embellish your drawing with colour, texture, detail and so on.

Mediated upside-down drawings

What you need:

a line drawing or print
drawing implements
paper

What to do:

1 Set the drawing to be copied upside down on the board or somewhere where good clear vision can be obtained by all.
2 Do not allow anyone to see the work right way up.
3 Set a reasonable time and allow everyone to draw what they see.
4 Stress the point that they are drawing in lines which are describing something.
5 When completed, turn the drawings up the right way to see how much better it may have been reproduced than had everyone tried to draw a known object right way up.

Perspective picture

What you need:

magazines
scissors
glue
paper
construction paper

What to do:

1 Using collage techniques from magazines or construction paper make up a foreground, middle ground, background and sky on your page - hills are usually the easiest way to do this.
2 Once this is glued down either cut or draw objects which are similar but are three different sizes, eg three people.
3 Position these on your landscape as they would be seen, ie a larger close-up photo of a person in the foreground and so on.

Magazine contour drawings

What you need:

magazines
scissors
glue
pens, pencils, paint etc
paper

What to do:

1 Cut out a large photograph from a magazine. This can be an object, scenery, food or whatever you like.
2 Fold the photograph in half and cut the picture straight down the centre.
3 Glue down one half of the photograph and discard the other.
4 Using drawing pencils try to reproduce the other side of the picture predicting from the half that you have.
5 Draw an outline or border around your picture.

language

builders
through
art
appreciation

A magazine file of ideas

What you need:

magazines
scissors
paste
folders
mounting cardboard

What to do:

1 Collect prints which stimulate thought and make good talking points for the class.
2 These can be backed with cardboard and kept for re-use.
3 Some suggested categories might be: warm colours, cool colours, contrasting colour, patterns, line, shape and spaces, architecture etc.

Art print ideas

What you need:

art posters or prints (exhibition adverts are a good source)
craft knives
backing cardboard
thick felt-tipped pens

How to use an art print

Puzzles: mount your print on heavy cardboard and cut it into pieces to make a jigsaw for discussion.
Information boards: cut out a lift-up flap from the print and mount it against white cardboard. Write in under the flap relevant information associated with the print.
Pop-up displays: mount your print onto cardboard. Cover the print with a cardboard sheet joined down one side so that you have made something similar to a card which opens to expose the print. Cut out lift-up flaps from the front sheet to display various sections of the print beneath. Invite the children to lift up a flap and predict what they think the print is about.

Games to play with slides and prints

Guessing game

1 Arrange a selection of prints for the class to see.
2 Choose a child to stand behind the class and give a description of one of the prints with reference to colour, texture and so on.
3 The child who guesses which print it is can now be in.

Musical art

1 Select an art print to stimulate feeling and discussion.
2 Ask the children to choose a group of instruments whose sounds they feel best reflect the mood of the print.
3 Compose a musical piece to represent the print.

Object arrangement

1 Have a collection of odds and ends in a box, eg toilet rolls, cardboard boxes etc.
2 Display a group of prints and ask a child to choose one.
3 The child must arrange the rubbish to make a junk sculpture which he feels

represents the print he has chosen.
4 The child who guesses which print it is and why, is in.

Write about it

1 Choose either an action print or a print containing people.
2 Ask the child to give the print a title of their own.
3 If an action print is being displayed, ask the child to write as though he were reporting a news item and to create the story and the facts.
4 If the print depicts people, ask the child to create a sequence of events for the people in the print that day and tell their story or history.

Make a sculpture come to life

1 Choose an appropriate sculpture for discussion (this may be a slide or a print of a sculpture or one that you have created yourself).
2 Tell the children to pretend that the sculpture is alive.
3 Ask the children to move the way they think the sculpture would or to make noises which reflect it.
4 Groups of children may wish to create a dance reflecting the sculpture.

Task card sources

Make up a collection of task cards with questions and activities which children can complete individually. Postcard size prints and magazine clips are a good source for these, though possibly the most useful are exhibition catalogues with full gloss prints which you can cut out and mount as you obtain both the print and the information.

recipe file

Translucent paper

What you need:

2 parts turpentine
1 part linseed oil
paper

What to do:

Brush over the paper and allow to dry.

Paste

What you need:

1/2 cup flour
water

What to do:

1 Add water to the flour and mix until you have thin paste.
2 Boil this mixture for 5 minutes, stirring constantly.
3 Add a few drops of peppermint to stop it from going mouldy.

Keep the paste in an airtight container.

Paint

Liquid starch paint

Simply pour over the page or add paint to it in a cup.

Soap powder paint

Mix the soap with a small amount of water until it becomes a smooth paste. Add dry powder paint and whip until stiff.

Finger paint

What you need:

1/2 cup cornstarch
1 litre boiling water
2 tablespoons glycerine

What to do:

1 Dissolve the starch in a little cold water.
2 Add boiling water gradually whilst stirring.
3 When clear, add glycerine to keep paint moist.
4 Store in an airtight container.

Powdered tempera or poster paint may be added for colour.

Liquid starch finger paint

What you need:

liquid starch
powder paint
paper

What to do:

1 Pour approximately 10 ml of liquid starch into the centre of the page.
2 Add some powder paint to the starch and work in together.

Wet paper is most effective for this activity.

Detergent paint

What you need:

detergent
powder paint

What to do:

1 Mix enough powder paint to liquid detergent to give a bright colour.
2 Use aluminium foil, glossy paper etc.

Natural dyes

Berries

What you need:

berries
water
strainer

What to do:

1 Crush berries and soak them overnight.
2 Boil the berries for approximately 1 hour then strain.
3 Use the liquid to make a dye bath.

Flowers

What you need:

blossoms and leaves such as rose petals, mint leaves etc
water
strainer

What to do:

1 Dry petals and leaves out in a well-ventilated area.
2 Boil for approximately 30 minutes then strain.
3 Use the liquid to make a dye bath.

Modelling recipes

Sawdust modelling dough

What you need:

2 cups sawdust
1 cup flour
liquid starch
10 ml glue

What to do:

Combine dry ingredients and moisten with starch, glue and water to gain a good modelling consistency.

Cornstarch dough

What you need:

2 cups table salt
1 cup cornstarch
1 cup water (warm if possible)

What to do:

1 Mix all the above ingredients and stir over a low heat until texture becomes firm.
2 Food colouring and oil can be added if you wish to have colours and more suppleness.

Non-hardening clay

What you need:

4 cups flour
1 cup salt
food colouring if required
about 200 ml of water
8 tablespoons vegetable oil

What to do:

Mix all the ingredients together. Store in an airtight container.

Crepe paper dough

What you need:

crepe paper (a variety of colours)
water
1 cup flour
liquid starch
10 ml glue

What to do:

1 Soak crepe paper in water overnight.
2 Drain and pour off the excess water.
3 Combine with remaining ingredients until a good modelling consistency is achieved.

Baker's clay

What you need:

4 cups flour
1 cup salt
1 1/2 cups water

What to do:

1 Mix all the ingredients together and knead as you would bread dough.
2 Add more water if necessary.
3 When modelled, this dough can be baked in an oven at 350° for approximately 40 minutes.

Papier mâché

Quick drying method

What you need:

4 cups pulp paper
a dessertspoon glue
1 cup plaster of Paris
water

What to do:

1 Soak paper pulp in water overnight.
2 Mix all the ingredients together until a modelling consistency is achieved.

Flour paste papier mâché

What you need:

newspaper
water
1/2 cup flour

What to do:

1 Soak torn newspapers overnight, then drain and squeeze out the excess water.
2 Add enough water to the flour to make a creamy consistency.
3 Boil this for approximately 5 minutes, stirring constantly to prevent lumps occurring.
4 Add to newspaper and model.

Collage

Paste

What you need:

2 cups flour
water

What to do:

1 Add enough water to the flour to give a creamy consistency.

Dough

What you need:

2 cups flour
2 cups salt
water

What to do:

1 Mix the dry ingredients together and blend in enough water to make a thin modelling mixture.
2 This can be used to cover card etc in order to secure shells and beads into it.

evaluation
checklist

Evaluation should be concerned with
children's growth rather than a perfect
piece of artwork. The following are lists
of concepts, skills and ideas for
evaluating art in the classroom.

Evaluation of the program

Does the unit:

- allow for the child's individuality?
- provide plenty of opportunity for exploration and experimentation of media?
- allow for the sequential development of the relevant art skills associated with the program?
- have activities which are within the child's range of capabilities?
- have activities which attempt to achieve the aims and objectives set down?
- provide a means of self-expression?
- provide experiences which bring joy and a positive self-concept to the child?

Evaluation of the artwork

- Does the artwork show originality?
- Is the artwork an expression of personal feeling?
- Does the artwork show a sense of harmony?
- Does the artwork demonstrate good use of the media provided?
- Is the artwork complete?
- Does the artwork show pride in work?
- Does the artwork show an understanding of the skills needed?

Evaluation of the child

Is the child able to:

- experiment with the media provided?
- show a proper knowledge and use of relevant art tools and equipment?
- take care of relevant art tools and media?
- use both tools and media in inventive ways?
- name relevant tools and media?
- demonstrate and make use of a growing art vocabulary?
- demonstrate an understanding of balance?
- incorporate a variety of techniques to embellish work?
- organise and arrange shapes in a pleasing way?
- self-motivate?
- adopt a receptive attitude and co-operate with others?
- participate well in groups?
- make independent judgements?
- recall the experience and express it verbally?
- participate freely in discussion?
- demonstrate increasing skill in problem solving?
- complete the given task?
- draw on previously acquired art skills in new tasks?
- demonstrate increasing aesthetic sense?
- show an appreciation of other classmates' efforts and differences?
- demonstrate enjoyment during art activities?
- demonstrate a self-analysis of their work?